SCiENCE SURPRiSES™

EVERYDAY PHYSICAL SCIENCE EXPERIMENTS WITH

GRAVITY

AMY FRENCH MERRILL

The Rosen Publishing Group's
PowerKids Press™
New York

For Amanda and Brittney

Some of the experiments in this book are designed for a child to do with an adult.

Published in 2002 by The Rosen Publishing Group, Inc.
29 East 21st Street, New York, NY 10010

First Edition

Book Design: Michael Caroleo and Michael de Guzman
Project Editor: Frances E. Ruffin

Photo Credits: p. 5 (Portraits of Newton and Galileo) © Bettmann/CORBIS; p. 5 (Earth and Moon) © PhotoDisc.
All experiment photos by Adriana Skura.

Merrill, Amy French.
Everyday physical science experiments with gravity / Amy French Merrill.
    p. cm. — (Science surprises)
Includes bibliographical references and index.
ISBN 0-8239-5805-1
1. Gravity—Experiments—Juvenile literature. [1. Gravity. 2. Gravity—Experiments. 3. Experiments.] I. Title. II. Series.
  QC178 .M455 2002
  531'.14'078—dc21

                                                                                                2001000954

Manufactured in the United States of America

CONTENTS

GOING UP, GOING DOWN

"What goes up must come down." We've heard this saying many times. What happens when you toss up a ball? In which direction do raindrops fall? Everything that goes up in the air comes back to the ground. Do you know why? Things fall to Earth because of **gravity**. Gravity holds us on the ground. Gravity holds the Moon in **orbit** around Earth. Gravity also holds Earth in orbit around the Sun.

In the 1500s and 1600s, scientists Galileo Galilei and Sir Isaac Newton discovered many things about the **physics** of gravity. Although scientists still do not know everything about how gravity works, they do know that gravity pulls **matter** together. Gravity is pulling on you and everything else on Earth all the time.

Gravity holds the Moon in orbit around Earth. Scientists Galileo Galilei (top) and Sir Isaac Newton (bottom) worked on experiments that have helped us to learn ▶ *about the physics of gravity.*

What Is Gravity?

Gravity is a **force**. A force is a push or a pull. You use forces every day. You use a lot of force when you push your bike up a hill, and a little force when you open a book. Some things are harder to push or pull than others. Here's how to make a force meter to test gravity. Measure and make a small hole 2 inches (5 cm) from the top of a piece of cardboard. Next measure and make two tiny holes that are 4 inches (10 cm) apart, below the first hole. Thread a rubber band through the top hole and wrap it around a pencil in the back of the cardboard. Thread small wire loops through the tiny holes.

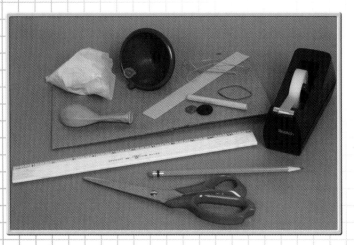

MATERIALS NEEDED:
rectangular piece of cardboard 3 by 12 inches (8 by 30 cm), rubber band, pencil, 2 pieces of wire 3 inches (8 cm), string 12 inches (30 cm), construction paper 8 inches (20 cm), glue, balloon, sand

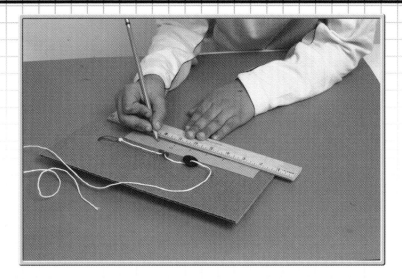

Thread a string through the first wire loop. Next thread the string through two small buttons and bring it through the bottom wire loop. Draw five short lines, all 1 inch (2.5 cm) apart, on a piece of construction paper. Label the lines on your scale 0 to 4. Line up the scale so that the button is level with the 0, then glue the scale to the cardboard. Tie a balloon full of sand to the free end of the string. How far does the rubber band stretch? **Experiment** with other objects.

There are many ways to test the force of gravity. You also can test its force by attaching a toy car ▶ to a string and pulling the car along a table.

Why Mass Matters

Did you know that every object in the world pulls on other objects? The strength of the pull depends on how much matter is in the objects. Scientists call the amount of matter in an object the object's **mass**. The more matter that objects have, the stronger the force of gravity between them will be. Most objects don't have enough matter in them to pull on each other for us to notice. You don't feel the pull of gravity between you and, say, a book. Earth has a lot of matter, though. The pull between Earth and other objects on Earth is strong. Try this experiment.

Find two objects, one heavier than the other, like a bowling ball and a tennis ball. Place the objects about 6 inches (15 cm) apart on

> **MATERIALS NEEDED:**
> two objects, one heavier than the other; a large piece of foam rubber (or a mattress); a marble

a large piece of foam rubber (or a mattress, if you're trying this at home). Place a marble on the foam rubber right in the middle of the two objects. Where does the marble go? The marble rolls toward the bowling ball, the heavier object, which has more matter.

WHAT IS WEIGHT?

Some objects are heavy, and some objects are light. When you measure how heavy or light something is, you are measuring its weight. Weight is the pull of gravity on an object. The pull of gravity on an object is just about the same all over Earth. For example, a kid who weighs 75 pounds (34 kg) in the United States will weigh the same in Spain, China, or anywhere else on Earth. If this 75-pound person traveled to the Moon, he or she would weigh 12 pounds (5 kg). Why? Earth is larger and has more matter than the Moon. Earth has six times the pull of gravity as the Moon! A 75-pound (34-kg) space traveler who

MATERIALS NEEDED:
scale, chart, paper, pencil, calculator

10

visited the even larger planet Saturn would weigh 175 pounds (79 kg) there, but would weigh only 3 pounds (1.4 kg) on the tiny planet of Pluto. Try **calculating** what the weight of different objects would be on the Moon. Make a chart. Label the first column "Objects." Label the second column "Weight on Earth" and the third column "Divide by 6." The last column is labeled "Weight on the Moon." Use a calculator, or have an adult help to find out what each object would weigh on Earth and on the Moon. Write the answers in your chart.

You might want to find out how much a 200-pound (9-kg) adult, a 45-pound (20-kg) dog, a 930-pound (422-kg) cow, a 6-pound (3-kg) backpack, and other objects would weigh on the Moon.

WHAT IS ACCELERATION?

When objects are put in motion, they usually don't stay at the same speed for very long. They eventually slow down or speed up. When objects speed up, they **accelerate**. Falling objects accelerate because of the pull of gravity. If two or more objects are dropped from the same height at the same time, they accelerate at the same rate of speed, no matter what they weigh. The higher the point from which things fall, however, the more they accelerate and the faster they travel.

Here's an experiment that demonstrates the second idea. Roll three pieces of clay into balls that are the same size. Working with

MATERIALS NEEDED:
Modeling clay in different colors

Falling objects accelerate because of the pull of gravity. ◀

an adult who can help you, drop one ball from a 7-foot (2.1-m) height onto an uncarpeted floor. Drop the second ball from a 5-foot (1.5-m) height, and drop the third ball from a 1½-foot (.5-m) height. Now turn over each ball of clay to see which is the flattest on the bottom. The ball that fell the greatest distance has the flattest bottom because it had more time to accelerate. When it hit the floor, it was traveling at a faster speed than the other balls.

Objects dropped from different heights hit the ground at different rates of acceleration. ▶

GRAVITY GAMES

What pulls you down a slide on a playground? Gravity, of course! You can experience the force of gravity during many games that you play.

Try this. Watch two friends toss a ball back and forth to each other. Watch the path of the ball in the air carefully. Ask your friends to try throwing the ball different ways—high, low, fast, or slow. What do you observe? Whether your friends toss high or low, fast or slow, the path of the ball is curved while it is in the air. The ball goes up when it's thrown, and then it comes back down. That's the force of gravity!

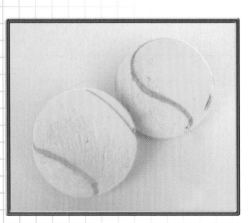

MATERIALS NEEDED:
two balls of equal size

14

◀ *Watch carefully as your friend tosses a ball. The path of the ball is curved while it is still in the air.*

Next try this. Hold two balls, one in each hand. At the same time, toss one ball forward, and let the other drop straight down. Which ball do you think will hit the ground first? Are you surprised? The balls hit the ground at the same time. The force of gravity acts the same on falling objects whether they are moving forward or falling straight down.

How would your favorite sport be different without gravity? ▶

Faking Gravity

You know that acceleration happens when an object picks up speed. When you are riding in a car and the driver presses on the gas pedal, you can feel the car accelerate, or move faster. As the car accelerates, you feel pushed back into your seat. The faster the car picks up speed, the harder a push you feel. The force you feel when riding in an accelerating car is very much the same as the force you feel when gravity pulls you to the ground. The forces of gravity and acceleration are the same.

To demonstrate this, hold a bucket of popped popcorn in one hand (or if you can, try this outdoors with a bucket of water). In one quick motion, swing the

> **Materials Needed:**
> bucket; 2 bags of plain, popped popcorn (or a bucketful of water)

Use oil- and butter-free popcorn for this experiment. Then the popcorn won't be sticky, and centrifugal force alone will keep it from falling out of the upside-down bucket.

bucket up and over your head in a circle. If you swing fast enough, the popcorn (or water) will not fall out. This is the result of **centrifugal force.** The force of the acceleration pushes the bucket's contents to the back of the container. Make sure you swing the bucket as fast as you can, stopping only when the bucket you're holding is in a down position.

You can experience centrifugal force on some amusement park rides. You still need a seat belt, though. ▶

CENTER OF GRAVITY

Earth's gravity pulls down on all parts of a person or an object. Have you ever watched tightrope walkers in a circus do their act? They have learned to balance themselves very well. Good balance comes from knowing where your **center of gravity** is. It is at the center of the body's mass. For people, the center of gravity is located at the waist. Tightrope walkers use a large pole to help keep them balanced. Here is an activity to help demonstrate how tightrope walkers keep their balance.

Twist the cap back onto an empty soda bottle. Make sure that it's tight. Now stick two forks into each side of a small

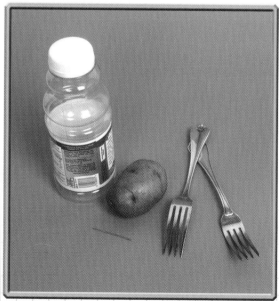

MATERIALS NEEDED:

plastic soda or juice bottle with a plastic cap, a small potato, a long needle, two forks

◀ This experiment also can be done using a bottle that has a cork.

potato. Have an adult help you to stick a long needle through the plastic bottle cap, leaving a ½ inch (1.3 cm) showing. Carefully place the potato with the forks on top of the sewing needle. Then watch as the potato and the forks are balanced on the tip of the needle.

The structure has a balancing point that is just below the center of gravity. Like a tightrope walker's pole, the forks serve as the balancing point that keeps the structure from tipping over.

The ends of the forks are just below the potato, which is the structure's center of gravity. If one fork tips over, the other fork balances it. ▶

Putting Gravity to Work

Gravity can be put to work for us in many ways. For example, the force of gravity will push water over a mountain to create a waterfall. A large waterfall can pour over a huge waterwheel in a power station to create electricity. This experiment demonstrates how a waterwheel works. Have an adult cut off the bottom of a plastic soda or juice bottle. Then punch holes in opposite sides of the bottle with a large nail. Next make the paddles for your waterwheel. Cut a sheet of stiff plastic into four pieces that are ½ by 2½ inches (1.3 by

MATERIALS NEEDED:

plastic soda or juice bottle, a cork, scissors, large nail, toothpicks, clay, small potato, rubber tubing, funnel, tape, sheet of stiff plastic, a bowl, colored water

6.4 cm). Cut four evenly spaced slits in a cork. Insert the plastic pieces into the cork. Push a toothpick in one end of the cork. Holding the wheel sideways, place the cork into the bottle so that the toothpick fits through one hole. Push a toothpick into the other end of the cork. Put clay at the ends of each toothpick for balance. Place the bottle upright into a bowl. Use strong tape to secure one end of the rubber tubing to the bottom of a funnel. Tape the other end of the tubing to the mouth of the bottle. Holding the funnel high, pour colored water into the funnel and the tubing. Watch gravity power your waterwheel.

Gravity and You

Astronauts traveling in a spacecraft float as if they are weightless because they and their spacecraft are actually in a condition of **free fall**. Their bodies feel a lot like yours does when you ride on a roller coaster that drops down a very steep hill. Floating around in space looks like a lot of fun, but it can actually make astronauts feel somewhat sick until their bodies adjust to having no gravity. Humans must have gravity to live. Your heart works by using the force of "push" to pump blood throughout your body. In space, weightlessness causes muscles and bones to get weak. Astronauts returning to Earth's gravity often have a hard time walking or even finding their balance for hours, even days! Scientists think that, someday, people may live in space. If that day comes, the people living on a space **colony** would need to have food, water, oxygen from air—and gravity!

GLOSSARY

accelerate (ek-SEH-luh-rayt) To increase in speed.

calculating (KAL-kyuhl-layt-ing) Finding out something, often by using math.

center of gravity (SEN-tur UV GRA-vih-tee) The point where the mass of a person or an object is concentrated, or thickest.

centrifugal force (sen-TRIH-fyuh-guhl FORS) The force that pushes outward on a turning or spinning object.

colony (KAH-luh-nee) A new place where people move, who are still ruled by the old country's leaders.

experiment (ik-SPER-uh-ment) To test something out.

force (FORS) Something that moves or pushes on something else.

free fall (FREE FAHL) The fall of a body as a result of gravity.

gravity (GRA-vih-tee) The force of attraction between matter.

mass (MAS) The amount of matter in something.

matter (MA-tur) The material that makes up something.

orbit (OR-bit) The circular path traveled by planets around the Sun.

physics (FIH-ziks) The scientific study of matter and energy and the laws that govern them. Physics is the study of motion, force, light, heat, sound, and electricity.

INDEX

WEB SITES

To learn more about gravity, check out this Web site:
www.brainpop.com/science/forces/gravity